MW00451622

How to Flirt with a Guy

A Girl's Guide to Being Flirtatious and Getting the Guy You Want

by Noah Kaleigh

Table of Contents

Introduction

Flirting is as natural and as rhythmic as dancing. And seeing as women are typically the more gifted sex when it comes to dancing, there's no reason why you shouldn't also rule the flirting game. And you do. Believe it or not, you are the ones who hold the power when it comes to flirting. This guide was written for the purpose of helping you learn how to use this power to have fun and to get the guy that you want.

Have you ever known a girl that seemed to mysteriously attract whatever man suited her fancy for the moment? She's able to do this because she knows how to flirt. When done properly, flirting can be used to guide men towards taking the actions you want them to take, whether it's asking for your number, asking you out on a date, or having them kiss or touch you. Flirting is a delicate process—you don't want to be too bold or direct. You want to keep it smooth. You want to allow the man you're pursuing the opportunity to feel the excitement of chasing you, so you have to keep things fun and subtle. In the following chapters, I'm going to provide you with a step-by-step flirting crash course that will have you primed to pursue the man of your dreams.

© Copyright 2015 by Miafn LLC - All rights reserved.

This document is geared towards providing reliable information in regards to the topic and issue covered. The publication is sold with the idea that the publisher is not required to render accounting, officially permitted, or otherwise, qualified services. If advice is necessary, legal or professional, a practiced individual in the profession should be ordered.

- From a Declaration of Principles which was accepted and approved equally by a Committee of the American Bar Association and a Committee of Publishers and Associations.

In no way is it legal to reproduce, duplicate, or transmit any part of this document in either electronic means or in printed format. Recording of this publication is strictly prohibited and any storage of this document is not allowed unless with written permission from the publisher. All rights reserved.

The information provided herein is stated to be truthful and consistent, in that any liability, in terms of inattention or otherwise, by any usage or abuse of any policies, processes, or directions contained within is solely and completely the responsibility of the recipient reader. Under no circumstances will any legal responsibility or blame be held against the publisher for any reparation, damages, or monetary loss due to the information herein, either directly or indirectly.

Respective authors own all copyrights not held by the publisher.

The information herein is offered for informational purposes solely, and is universal as so. The presentation of the information is without contract or any type of guarantee assurance.

The trademarks that are used are without any consent, and the publication of the trademark is without permission or backing by the trademark owner. All trademarks and brands within this book are for clarifying purposes only and are the owned by the owners themselves, not affiliated with this document.

3

Chapter 1: The Fundamentals of Flirting

Flirting is always the first step in courtship. Consider a married couple that's been together for over 50 years. Their first ever romantic interaction was based in a flirtatious exchange. Flirtation is the first impression of romance and vice versa. It's important you know how to do it well.

For women, the art of flirtation is the art of subtly allowing and inviting the man to take action. A guy is risking the wellbeing of his precious ego when he flirts with a girl. If his advances are unwelcome, then he could be labeled a creep or a pervert, and the world will show him no sympathy. Most men will not proceed without your prompts. In this chapter, we'll examine the fundamentals of being a good flirt.

It all begins with a warm climate, not temperature-wise, but personality-wise. When you want a guy to feel comfortable enough to flirt with you, you need to be radiating with warmth and openness when he's around you. Smiling is a good start. Add a dash of coyness and humor, and you'll be setting the right tone. It's also ok to be a little bashful when he compliments you. This will show him that you appreciate his overtures and care about his opinions.

A good way to initiate a flirtatious interaction with a guy is to feed his ego and confidence. Tell him you like what he's wearing, or the way he did his hair. Tell him you were impressed by his performance at the track meet or basketball game. If he's not an athlete, find some other way to complement him that lets him know you're interested in his pursuits and that you notice him. You're still in a relatively low risk position, and if he doesn't start to reciprocate your warmness, then you can just write off the interaction as harmless small talk.

Another flirting fundamental is initiating and maintaining eye contact. Don't just stare blankly at him, but *engage* him with your eyes. Try to pair your sustained eye contact with sustained attention. Don't get caught up in your own head but focus instead on the simple pleasure of being around him. If you get a little nervous, that's ok too. Flirting is not a staring contest, but making good eye contact can go a long way towards building an emotional connection with a guy.

Women who flirt well are masterful with their expressions. They know how to puff out their bottom lip when they want to look pouty. They know when to tuck their hair behind their ears to look coy or nervous (in a cute way). They know how to giggle and how to laugh. They know how to telegraph mischievousness with their eyes. These are skills that you can learn if you don't feel you possess them innately. Practice flirty expressions in front of your mirror. Learn how to make faces that make you look cute. Learn how to make faces that make you look sexy. Being a master of your expressions will make you more naturally flirtatious and will also help you improve your confidence and poise.

Another fundamental aspect of flirting is the art of teasing. Good flirts are always lighthearted and know exactly when to tease the guy they're after. No one responds well to the girl who has no sense of sarcasm or wit. Nor to one who blandly praises away at the guy she's trying to flirt with, and is left to wonder why he doesn't respond. It's ok to tease. It's ok to give him a hard time about stuff when he deserves it, or even when he doesn't. Therefore, as long as you're light-hearted about it and teasing in good fun with underlying warmth, then you'll be much more enjoyable for him to flirt with. So find ways to give him a hard time and watch him try and back-peddle and strain his way into your good graces.

You can be proactive in your flirting without being obnoxious, brash, or obvious. It's important to be able to be both playful and feminine at the same time. Keep your voice soft, your attire cute, and your demeanor subtle. For a guy, flirting with a mysterious and feminine woman is much more exciting than flirting with a girl who's too brazen and over the top. A well-calibrated flirt is girly and vulnerable, but also subtle. Men are programmed to want to be protectors, and even if you don't think of yourself as a girly girl, being more feminine will allow you to satisfy a man's evolutionary itch.

Another fundamental element of good flirtation skills involves finding ways to integrate "touch" into your interactions. A good way to get your touch game going is to think of wanting to touch a guy you like as a natural urge. Don't overthink it or hesitate, whenever you feel like touching him, touch him. You will be able to judge from his response whether he's digging you or not, and if he's not, no harm no foul. If he *is* digging you, then he'll probably find a way to touch you back.

So now that you have the fundamentals down, it's time to go out into the field and get some real flirting experience. There's a multitude of different ways to orchestrate opportunities to flirt. We'll break them down in the following chapters.

Chapter 2: How to Grab Him by the Five Senses

Without sensual undertones, flirting ceases to be flirting and becomes just talking or hanging out, which isn't the road you want to be on if you're looking to be more than friends. Flirting with a guy requires you to move an interaction to a sensual plane, and you do this by appealing to one or more of his senses. When a woman lets her hair down, its flowing texture evokes the sense of touch. A man imagines running his fingers through that luscious hair and holding her by the head as he goes in for a passionate kiss. Romance, even at its earliest stages, requires the opportunity for these types of fantasies to flourish. When flirting with a guy, you should enroll as many of his senses as possible in order to get his attention. Here's how you do it:

Flirting by Sight

You don't have to dress like a Vegas hooker to be sexy and alluring, but you do want him to see you as sensually alluring and mysterious, someone he's dying to get to know. Remember, you want to flirt with *him*, not *everyone in the room*. Rather than wearing a shirt with a bare mid-riff, show him your belly button and ask him whether you should get a belly button ring. Show him your ankle, leg, or shoulder and tell him you've been considering getting a tattoo. Giving him a private peek at your PG-13 rated erogenous zones will be both visually sensual for him, and it will also start a conversation.

If you're walking by a guy you're interested in, try turning your head slowly halfway towards him and stare for a few seconds. Be prepared for him to catch you – this is what you want—and when it happens, shoot him a confident smile.

If he's across the room from you in a coffee shop, bar or elsewhere, use your legs to your advantage. Men are inclined to focus on movement, so get his attention by crossing your legs and moving your foot in a circular motion. Doing this will draw his eyes to your sexy legs and get his motor humming. Another good across-the-room flirting technique that works especially well in coffee shops is to dip your finger in your dessert or latte foam and then lick it off. You'll definitely attract some curious and possibly smitten stares with this tactic, and a guy should read this as a cue that you're open to being approached. Another variation is to lick the rim of your beer or espresso mug with the tip of your tongue. These flirtation techniques don't have to be over-the-top to the point where they're comical. Keep them subtle and simple.

Speaking of subtle and simple, flirting by sight can also be effective when you're direct. One sure-fire way to let a guy know you're interested is by not breaking your stare after he catches you looking at him. Instead, give him a nice once-over, looking him over from bottom to top until you meet his eyes with a slight smile. Hold his gaze for a total of three seconds, then bite the corner of your lip and look down. If you've got a conversation going, pick an opportune moment and lean in close to him until you're within a few inches from his face, linger there for a few beats, then steadily return. If he's thinking about how much he wants to kiss you, then you should be able to read it on his face.

Eye contact is good, but keep it rhythmic, off-and-on. Too much eye contact can smother out the fires of passion. It's important for a woman to maintain her mystery, especially in the early phases of flirting.

Flirting by Touch

In the flirting game, touching is where the rubber meets the road. Using your flirting skills to make physical contact with a guy should tip him off to the fact that you're interested in him.

Flirting by touch can commence immediately after you meet a guy whom you'd like to get to know better. When you shake his hand, wrap your other hand over his and hold it, letting the grip linger for a brief moment longer than you'd allow for an ordinary handshake. If you're sitting with him at a table or at bar, you can let him know that you're comfortable with him by placing the back of your hand on your knee, palm-up or by placing your hand palm-up on the table or bar. This body-language will inspire him to take your hand if he's feeling bold. Don't be afraid to take the lead in touching. During a conversation, try touching his leg or arm for emphasis on a point you're making or to highlight a funny story you're telling him. Another great way to initiate some flirtatious touching in the middle of a conversation is to ask him if it's hot or cold and take his hand and place it on your forehead.

Another great way to initiate sensual touching, ideally in a more private environment, is to talk your way into a massage. You can do this by directing the conversation to the subject of massages, how much you enjoy receiving them, giving them etc. You can also grab your shoulder and sigh, prompting him to ask what's wrong and then telling him your shoulder feels a little tense while you stare longingly into his eyes, quietly and sensually begging for him to touch you.

The palm-reader routine is another great way to induce flirtatious touching while on the hunt. Hold his hand and trace the lines in on his palm, tell him he's soon to have a passionate encounter with a mysterious, sexy, and amazing woman he has just met.

Give him a big hug for no reason in particular, just out of the blue, even if you don't know him. If that's too random for you, find a reason, maybe you're just so happy to have found out that Pluto has been officially reinstated as a planet and is no longer denigrated to being merely an escaped moon of Neptune. If you'd prefer a more subtle approach, when you're walking through a crowded room, touch his lower back as you walk by or steady yourself using his shoulder or bicep as a grip.

Flirting by Sound

The tone and texture of your voice can go a long way in your flirting game. It's not always so much about what you say, but how you say it and how it inspires his imagination.

A lot of women (and men) are turned off by bars and clubs because the noise level interferes with their ability to communicate verbally. One way to make the best of a loud room is to use it to justify a close quarters conversation. Lean in slowly to speak to him, just outside of his ear to a point where the two of you are nearly cheek to cheek. Speak slowly and clearly, not too loudly; he'll hear you if you're right next to his ear.

It's also fun to flirt over the phone. If the two of you are talking on the phone, then you've (hopefully) already given him your number, and you can be a little more open about your interest in him. You can tell stories about past romantic encounters and make sexy innuendoes or jokes. You can also tease back and forth, calling out your guy and giving him a hard time about little things. If he gets fired up and playfully defensive, then you're doing a good job!

Another thing about guys - they love to hear their own names. Look for opportunities to flirtatiously use his name. For example, if he tells you a sad story, say: "Poor Johnny, that sounds awful." Or, if you're moving in for the kill, lean over to him and say, "You know Johnny, I love men who ..." and tell him what you like about him.

Flirting by Smell

Smelling delectable will make you even more of a formidable flirting force. Find a fragrance that gives you confidence and makes you feel sexy, and then let it work for you. A great tactic is to tell a guy that you're trying out a new perfume and would like his opinion, then hold out your wrist and let him take it in.

If a guy's smell catches your attention, don't miss the opportunity to flirtatiously capitalize. Move in closer to him and let him know how much his smell turns you on. If you don't know him that well yet, then play it a little more subtly. Make a comment about his fragrance that's half tease, half compliment like "Wow, someone smells nice and all dolled up for the ladies."

Flirting by Taste

Using a man's taste buds as a way to his heart is among the sweetest forms of flirtation. Baking a guy a batch of cookies or some other sensual culinary creation is a great way of showing him that you kinda dig him. Flirting by way of food works well in more professional and tame environments, like the office or at school.

Grabbing him by the senses is a powerful and visceral way to telegraph your interest and get his imagination going. But the five basic senses aren't our only means of flirtatious communication. Basic body language also plays a huge role in the mating dance. When you're flirting with someone, you should try to keep yourself openly aligned with them, chest-to-chest. In other words, don't shield yourself with your arms, back, or shoulders. If you're sitting at a bar, keep your arm (nearest the guy with whom you're flirting) at your side and turn your body some to face him. Play with your hair a little from time to time, not so much that you look nervous, but in a coy and sensual way. Keep smiling and keep the conversation light and fun.

Chapter 3: Flirting by Way of Instigation

If you want to become a master flirter, then you need to be able to instigate situations – by way of flirtation – that lead to *even more* flirtation. The most successful women employ multiple methods of flirting, using all of their assets and always capitalizing on a situation once it presents itself. In this chapter we'll go over a few commonplace instigation strategies that can be attempted by almost any would-be flirter.

At a party, if you want to get the attention of a certain someone, set yourself apart from the crowd by sitting or standing in an unusual but visible place. Maybe out on the deck, or up on a table or the counter. If you can locate a nice high perch somewhere, ask the guy you're interested in to lift you up so you can reach it. Another way to get his attention at a party is to stand on your tip-toes and look over the room, making sure that he notices you. Tell him that you're unable to spot your friends, and that you're all alone. If he's interested in you, he'll let you know by starting a conversation.

One other tried-and-tested tactic to make yourself stand out at a party is to take over as the bar tender, mix your signature cocktail or try something crazy and reckless and make him your honorary taste-tester. Whether it's good, bad, or ugly, your drink will make for a fine introductory conversation piece. Another way to be pro-active with your flirting is to ask him if he wouldn't mind guarding the door to the restroom while you use it. Speaking of doors, try mingling by the front of door at the next party you attend. Hang out in a place where you're among the first to see new arrivals. When the guy that you've been waiting for arrives, sigh with relief as you tell him coyly "Hey! I've been waiting for someone interesting to show up!" If there's a guy you're interested in, someone who's a bit socially awkward at parties or looks a little lost, then go up to him and tell him that you've been sent by the "Good Time Alliance Insurance Company" (or some other fictional agency) and you're there to make ensure he doesn't have a boring night. If that doesn't get the guy at least curious about you, then he probably doesn't have a pulse.

A lot of the same flirting techniques you'd use at a house party can also be used at a bar. The bar scene is a little more controlled. You can't sit on the tables, make your own drinks, and sometimes, due to noise levels, you'll have limited ability even to converse. But that doesn't mean that the bar or club can't be a fine venue in which to flex your flirt muscles. Standing out in a bar isn't hard. If you want someone to talk to you, simply bring in a sketch pad or your laptop, and you'll have an easy conversation starter. Better yet, take the driver's seat. If you find the guy you want to talk to at the bar, sit down next to him and ask: "Have you ever been approached by a complete stranger?" If the bar is crowded and the bar tenders are furiously filling orders, slip some money in his hands and ask if he'd mind ordering you a drink. Disappear for a few minutes, come back, and see what happens. Another approach: tell him you'll buy him a drink but he's going to have to repay you with an interesting conversation. Or, you could order two drinks and offer one to the guy whom you wish to flirt with. Explain to him that the bartender accidentally gave you two drinks and you'd like him to take one off your hands so you don't get too wasted. Remember to work noisy venues to your advantage— this applies especially to bars and clubs – by using your body language, pulling him in close to you, or talking cheek to cheek in your sexiest voice.

If the bar or club (or any venue) you're at has a line outside, then you can start a conversation easily with a cute guy by asking him if he thinks the venue is worth the wait. If you can avoid it, try not to discuss the weather. Always be on the look- out for props you can use to aid your flirting efforts. Cell phones are great. Take out your phone and snap a picture of your cute guy, and tell him you wanted proof that you saw the hottest guy in town. Another cell-phone assisted flirting method is to take his phone and look it over.

Look up at him gravely and say the phone doesn't suit him. When he asks why, tell him because it's missing a key component, your phone number!

Guys love sports, so whether you're at a bar, club, or grocery store, one approach that uses flattery while stimulating conversation is to tell a guy that he looks like an athlete and to ask him what sport he likes to play. Speaking of athletics, the gym is a great place to complement a guy on his sporting physique. There are a variety of tactics you can use to flirtatiously instigate at the gym. If there are rows of empty treadmills, choose the one right next to the guy you're digging. He should get the hint. You can start a conversation with a buff guy at the gym by saying "Hey it looks like *you* spend a lot of time here, do you mind showing me around?" If you want to flirt with you aerobics instructor, ask him to spend a little more time with you after class perfecting your moves.

Opportunities to flirt are everywhere, including right at your front door. Need a lightbulb changed, or maybe you want to mount a shelf, or, if you're really girly, maybe you need someone to come kill a spider - - see if your sexy neighbor is up for the task. Reward him with a beer and invite him to stay a while. Trouble with your car? Need I say more?

Chapter 4: Making Yourself More "Flirtable"

In order to have a chance to flirt, you have to establish some level of décor with the guy you hope to flirt with. He either has to approach you, or you have to already know one another through mutual friends. If you're looking to expand your range of potential flirting partners, then you need to work on making yourself more "flirtable." Here's how you do it.

The Approachability Factor

In order to flirt, you must interact. And before you can interact, you must approach or be approached. Moreover, considering that most women would rather have a guy approach them than vice versa, it falls on you to make yourself approachable.

The way you dress, of course, plays a huge role in determining who's going to try and flirt with you and when. If you're going out during the day, try dressing down a bit. You'll be more likely to be approached by a handsome stranger at a coffee shop if you're dressed in a more subdued and down-to-earth fashion. If it's a nighttime venue, then of course, by all means come out dressed to the hilt, eyes bright and guns blazing.

Another variable that factors into your approachability is how engaged you are in whatever you're doing. If you go out to the coffee shop with a book you really love, you'll be more likely to be approached while lost between its pages than you'd be if you were staring around aimlessly. The idea here is to be approachable without looking desperate or needy. So be sure to get a book that you really dig, or bring your lap top and work on a project that really captures your attention. Guys will pick up on the fact that you're captivated and will naturally want to ask "what's going on!?"

Go out alone. Women are much easier for guys to talk to if they're out by themselves rather than amidst a tribe of other females (or males). Instead of bringing out your BFF, bring along your laptop. If you're lucky, you may make a new friend whilst out and about. Also, stay put when you're out. Pick a table or a seat at a bar and stay, don't migrate around. Sometimes it takes guys a while to work up the nerve to strike up a random conversation with a woman they're attracted to. To help set guys more at ease, choose smaller venues. Guys, with their oh-so-fragile egos, are apt to worry about the possibility of striking out in front of large groups of people. Small bakeries, coffee shops and bars may prove more comfortable spots for men to approach you.

Don't burden yourself with expectations. You may be approached or you may not be. If you feel that you need guys to try and flirt with you in order to feel validated, then you probably have some serious work to do on building your own self-esteem. Try to remember that for every 10 guys who see you and would like to approach you, only one of them will end up doing so. And there are a variety of reasons for this. Maybe the guy doesn't feel he's in the right mood for a chat with a random woman. Maybe he doesn't have the time. Maybe he has a girlfriend. Don't take it personally and don't rush it. It will happen when it happens.

Practice Makes Perfect

Practice makes perfect and success breeds success. You'll find that they come in waves. No one will talk to you for weeks and then one day you'll be at the coffee shop and 4 guys will flirt with you back to back, and maybe two of them will end up asking for your number. Get as much flirting practice under your belt as possible. The more you do it, the better you'll get at it. When guys see you flirting with other guys, it will spark their competitive drive and affirm in their minds that you're someone who must be fun to talk to.

Watch for Buying Signals and Respond

A savvy flirter knows when it's "game on." There are several ways to tell when a guy is really flirting with you. If he attempts to stand out from other guys, being the leader in his group or talking down a guy he sees as a potential rival for your affections, then he's trying to flirt with you. He may also puff out his chest or adjust his posture to a more upright and alpha state.

If he goes out of his way to tell you something impressive about himself, like how successful he is in his career or all the time he spends volunteering at the animal shelter, then it's safe to say that he's trying to flirt with you. Your response to these volleys of flirtation should be attentive and admiring, but also light-hearted and teasing. Speaking of teasing, if a guy you don't know that well insists on teasing you relentlessly, then he's definitely flirting with you. In a situation like this, it's much better to be teased than to be ignored. Also, watch for accidental touches and eye contact, both are sure signs of flirtatious intentions. When you recognize these and other signs, deploy any of the flirting routines described in the previous chapters and, most importantly, have fun!

Conclusion

One of the main reasons women seek help in "learning how to flirt" is that they lack the confidence that makes flirting come naturally and easily. Practicing the techniques in this book will especially help those who aren't naturally confident or comfortable with flirting. Also, by practicing these methods and having fun with them, you will come to realize your power to attract others and may begin to feel more confident in general when hanging around guys (and girls as well). As was noted in Chapter 4, success breeds success. Once you get comfortable flirting, you will come across as more attractive and more confident. Most importantly, keep trying and don't get discouraged by an awkward moment or two. It's ok to fall on your face from time to time so long as you get back up.

To be a good flirt you must be willing to be a little vulnerable. To do this you need to adopt a carefree, don't-give-a-damn attitude, at least temporarily. In most environments conducive to flirting, like parties or clubs, people are there to have fun. To thrive in these types of social environments, having a light heart is essential. Don't fall apart and run home the moment a guy you dig doesn't respond to your flirtation efforts. Maybe he's got a girlfriend at home, a kid even. Maybe he knows that if he indulges you, it will send him down a dangerous road, especially given how sexy and irresistible you are. Maybe he's gay, or in a bad mood that day, or socially awkward, or maybe he's just not interested in you. The point is that it doesn't really matter. Pick up and move on. The more you flirt the better you'll get at it, so flirt early and often. Make it a part of your personality.

Finally, I'd like to thank you for purchasing this book! If you enjoyed it or found it helpful, I'd greatly appreciate it if you'd take a moment to leave a review on Amazon. Thank you!